So What

A Single Mom's* Guide to Staying Sane in the 21st Century

* Not just for single moms

Laynee Gilbert

For Supriya~
Where the journey
began!
Best wishes,
Laynee
Liana

L.O.A. Publications

Cover art by Liana.
Cover design by Jeff Boissier.

Printed by Signature Book Printing, www.sbpbooks.com

First edition published 2012 by L.O.A. Publications.

Library of Congress Control Number: 2011910603

L.O.A. Publications
P.O. Box 6107
San Jose, California 95150-6107
LOApubs@aol.com
www.loapublications.com

ISBN 10:   0-9678966-3-0
ISBN 13:   978-0-9678966-3-2

Other books by Laynee Gilbert:
The Complete Dream Journal
I Remember You: A Grief Journal
Pass It On: Ultimate Reflections on Life and Death
Precious Companion: A Book of Comfort and Remembrance After the Loss of a Pet

For Liana, my joy

Contents

Introduction

I'd had quite a year. Depending on what day you started counting, in the course of one year I divorced my husband, packed up and sold our house, bought and moved into another, lived in a small hotel room for three weeks in between homes with my then 7-year-old daughter and our three cats, grieved the loss of a dear family friend, lunged into life as a single mother working full-time both outside and inside the home, and then topped it all off with emergency surgery to replace a couple of disks in my neck (but not in time to prevent nerve damage to my left arm).

Breathe.

The whole time, I barely missed a beat. Life goes on, have to take care of my daughter first. Get her up and going in the morning, make sure there's ample food for breakfast and healthy food in her lunch bag, drive her across town to school and then another half hour in traffic to work, juggle appointments with doctors and dentists between management and meetings, pick her up and take her to karate or music lessons, enter the night-time routine of dinner, dishes, homework, bath, bedtime. Oh, and be sure to have lots of quality time with her.

Although I said I barely missed a beat, at one point near the end of that year something snapped inside. In a good way. One evening, during the usual fourth or fifth ugly battle with my daughter about something gravely important like brushing her teeth, suddenly the words *So What* popped into my head. *So What* if she doesn't brush her teeth tonight. *So What* if she sleeps on the couch instead of in her bed. *So What* if she doesn't complete every single page of her homework. *So What.* I stopped mid-stream in our battle and just... wait for it... gave in. Yes, that's right, I said OK to her not having to brush her teeth, OK to her sleeping on the couch, and even OK to her watching one more television program before she went to bed (and I actually sat down and watched with her). And you know what? The earth didn't stop revolving. She didn't turn into a monster. Instead, we shared a very pleasant rest of the evening together, the best we'd had in a long time.

I learned something deeply profound that night, and I've been consciously practicing it ever since. It's no great theory of enlightenment that will take years of study. It's simply the power of these two words: *So What.*

Now, it's important to understand the intended meaning of these two words as used in the context of this book. Stated with a cynical edge in the voice and a drop in pitch, "*So What*" implies, "Who cares?" But when stated with an upward shift of tone after a nice deep breath, "*So What*" suggests, "Is this *really* such a big deal?" What awful thing will happen if I let go of trying to control this and allow it to just be? Anyone who knows me knows I would never adopt a negative attitude of "who cares". I care so deeply about people and animals and the home we call planet earth, caring is not part of the equation.

It's not about Caring; it's about Controlling.

When I apply the *So What* attitude, I am not caring any less, I'm merely surrendering in a positive way and letting go of trying to control all outcomes. My daughter doesn't question for a moment my level of caring. She knows I care desperately about her health, happiness and well-being. I've just found a new way of doing so without driving us both nuts.

The more I practice this fresh approach to parenting and self-preservation, the stronger our relationship becomes. And that's what this book is all about.

****

Before moving on, I feel compelled to say that I'm fully aware of the relative good fortune I have in my life, as compared to many other single moms who have it so much harder. There was a woman I once worked with at a highly demanding startup company, a single mother of four ranging in age from teen to toddler. Each child had medical and/or social challenges that required a great deal of attention. Nevertheless, this woman still managed to come to work each day and get the job done. She was incredibly stressed and it leaked out occasionally, but from my perspective she was Wonder Woman.

Although it's good to pause and count our blessings, comparing ourselves to others we view as less fortunate too often results in dismissing or condemning ourselves when we start buckling under the pressure. We need to acknowledge and respect our own anxiety and challenges, and freely pat ourselves on the back for our daily super-heroic accomplishments!

Additionally, I wholly recognize these same stressful life challenges exist not just for single moms, but also for married moms and for dads as well... and yes, even for men and women without any kids at all. But the inspiration for this book was born from my own experience as a single mom, so that's why the title stands.

Although I spent more than 20 years in private practice as a licensed marriage, family and child counselor, this book is not intended as a professional treatise. Rather, it's written from my own humble perspective gleaned from the trenches of parenthood. One person's story can never speak for all. Take what fits and leave the rest, and find comfort in the fact that you're far from alone in your personal quest for sanity.

P.S. My child is only eight. With all the lessons yet to come, I'm sure I'll be writing a sequel when she's 15, if not sooner!

1.

The Art and Heart of *So What*

I am what some people refer to as a late-in-life mom. I was in my 40's when I adopted my daughter, which makes me the same age as some of her peers' grandparents. This means I was raised in a world without cell phones, laptops and the Internet, where doing a school research project required opening the *Encyclopedia Britannica* or actually going to the library. Television carried only seven stations and the most risqué shows to do battle over were *Laugh-In* and *Love American Style*. My mom didn't have another job outside of the home, so her primary focus was on maintaining the perfect house, making sure dinner was on the table every night when Dad came home from work, and shaping her kids to be Perfect as her default primary measure of success. "What will people think" was the motto that ruled the roost. Divorce was something shameful spoken about in hushed tones, and I rarely met a woman in the role of single mom.

Enter the 21st century. A new genre of battles arise such as how old my daughter has to be to get an iPod and cell phone, how much time she can spend on the Internet surfing or chatting, which TV shows she can watch out of the kazillion choices offered 24x7. I'm pulled in multiple directions handling a full-time paid job in addition to my full-time parenting job. According to my deeply embedded inner critic, I'm supposed to be this perfect mom (albeit divorced and single) setting perfect boundaries and establishing perfect values that will launch my daughter into her own perfect life. But the road map I was raised with has become relatively obsolete, and the word "perfection" has become an utter conundrum. Echoes of my late mom's voice persist, nagging at me whenever I fail to live up to her standards (which is pretty much commonplace). I've come to recognize that in my battles with my daughter, I'm doing battle with my internalized mom at the same time, snapping at her to get out of the way so I can deal with this myself. Remarkably, with *So What*, I've found a way to drop the battle on both fronts.

So, What is So What*?*

So What is not a cognitive-behavioral technique that's been proven with scientific or empirical research.

So What is an art, not a science.

It's about learning how to let go of both the inner and outer struggle.

It's about forgiveness of imperfection.

It's about letting go of some (not all) control.

It's about letting go of fear and guilt – emotions rooted in the illusion of the future and remnants of the past.

It's about coming back to the here-and-now, to what's real.

Ultimately, it's about fostering that precious bond between you and your child.

When the day-to-day stuff of life derails us, *So What* helps to restore our sanity and get us back on track.

Every *So What*, every one, invites a decision. All day long, life presents us with situations that require us to weigh alternatives. How am I going to deal with *this* one? How am I going to deal with *that*? As my daughter gets older and her ideas and behavior become more complex, the *So What* decisions become more and more challenging. With each one, I need to ask myself: In this moment, how critical is this? How important is this in the big picture?

What is my best possible response right now, balancing the needs of my child, our relationship and myself?

At the heart of *So What* is the awareness and ability to tap into our own creative energy, so as to effectively evaluate and address these multi-dimensional needs in any given situation. There is never a shortage of opportunities to practice.

One night at our favorite ice cream store, I spied my young daughter secretly pick up an M&M off the ground and put it in her mouth. YUCK! How AWFUL! After dramatically detailing all the reasons why she should never again even THINK about doing something so disgusting and dangerous (while simultaneously taking a mental inventory of witnesses), I was stopped in my tracks by the dreadful, ashamed look on her face. I paused and reflected for a moment...

Yes, a lesson needed to be taught, but not through intolerance and shame.

Then the words *So What* drifted into consciousness. Does it really have to be *that* big of a deal? A young child doesn't think about all the germs and grossness of eating somebody else's candy off the ground. They just see the pretty bright colors and imagine the sweetness in their mouth. Was that really going to kill her? Odds are strongly against it. No major crime had been committed. This was simply an innocent, impulsive act of a child, and how I respond is between her and me – it's inconsequential if anyone else is observing us. I took a deep breath... and then apologized to her for having reacted so harshly, adding, "When I was your age, I probably would've done the same thing." Instantly, the energy shifted and we exchanged gentle, loving smiles. Although it was a bit delayed, I'm grateful *So What* came to my aid in time. The apology and self-disclosure rescued the evening, and went a long way toward strengthening our relationship and building her self-esteem.

A great relationship can't happen without an open line of communication, and an open line of communication requires ultimate trust that each person can be who they are, say what they need to say – *even make mistakes* – without being attacked or confronted with closed-minded harsh judgment in response. As a parent, I need to get a grip on my own personal triggers so that I can respond evenly and authentically with my child. Even if I lose my patience (which is a given, I'm only human), or if something else disrupts our equilibrium, what's key is that at the end of the day we're okay again. Otherwise, bricks slowly pile up, until one day there's an impenetrable wall.

2.

Buttons and Hooks

There's no one, universal thing that drives all parents over the edge. We each have our own special buttons or hot spots that turn the world red when pushed, and hooks that automatically evoke the same old self-defeating, repetitive knee-jerk responses. Fundamental to *So What* is learning how to recognize and defuse these buttons and hooks, empowering us to respond in a unique, genuine, in-the-moment way.

I humbly admit that my personal audit of buttons and hooks has resulted in a relatively long list (and these are just the highlights). On the bright side, I've provided lots of examples for parallel parking! As you read through this list, take note of your own buttons and hooks. Identifying them is the first step toward defusing them.

Piles

High on my list of buttons is Piles.

By nature, I prefer to maintain an orderly,

uncluttered environment. My external physical environment has a direct impact on my internal mental environment. The less chaos on the outside, the more calm on the inside.

My daughter is the complete opposite. She loves every space filled, and piles to her are a great way to view all of her treasures at all times.

Predictably, "clean-up time" was one of our daily battles.

I was operating on the need to pick up everything each day to keep things from accumulating out of control. She was operating on the need to play. A funny thing happened when I snapped and started practicing *So What*. I let the piles go a day, then two, and then a whole week. And you know what? It didn't get completely out of control. It only took about an hour out of the weekend to get everything back into place (reasonably). What's more, I didn't freak out about the piles starting all over again five minutes later when she proceeded to take all the blankets out of the closet for the umpteenth time to create another cool fort. Deep breath, *So What*. We'll pick them up again next weekend.

What I'm discovering by releasing little bits at a time is that I haven't gotten completely buried, and life hasn't gotten completely out of control. There are times when I reach the point of "enough is enough" and we have our cleanup day or whatever may be needed, but it doesn't pack the same intensity of feeling that it used to. We just get the job done. In fact, I'm a bit reluctant to admit it, but I've even come to appreciate her piles in a new way, to see them as comfort instead of clutter, and I'm not so uptight between pick-ups.

Lightening up on her piles has generalized to being able to lighten up some on my own. Amazingly, it's no longer a given that I'll get all the dishes done before I go to bed! Most of the time I still do (this isn't magic, I'm still a highly compulsive and hyper-responsible person by nature), but sometimes it's midnight or later when I'm finally done with my parenting and work responsibilities, and I still haven't finished cleaning up the dishes from dinner... and *So What* if I have some extra dishes to deal with in the morning or even if they have to wait longer. You know what? They still get done eventually.

Letting go of some *control is not a slippery slope to letting go of* all *control.*

We can let go of *some* control and still keep it together. True, my house in general is a bit messier than I would like it to be, with little piles adorning most corners and trimming the woodwork, but *So What*. My daughter and cats don't seem to mind, and I'm learning to live with it as well.

The Pack Rat

Related to Piles is the Pack Rat. My personal philosophy is that if I haven't worn or used something in a year or two, then donate it to someone who can put it to use. Prior to parenthood, there was plenty of room in my attic or basement. Not anymore. My daughter cannot let go of her toys or clothes. Ever. She likely has more than 100 stuffed animals accumulated over her relatively short lifetime. I wanted to go through them and give some away, but she wouldn't hear of it. She insisted they were all equally precious to her, and I could see she was poised to protect them at all costs. I tried to logic with her but couldn't penetrate an inch, she was steadfast in her position. As my knee threatened to kick off yet another round of pointless sparring, I stopped. *So What*. There's still room in the attic. I don't have to be in a hurry.

A similar pattern would occur every year around holiday time, when I felt it was more important than ever to teach her about giving to those less fortunate than herself, with the added advantage of making room in her closet for the new toys and clothes to come. Last year she was so proud of herself for gathering together what I considered a measly few items to donate, and regrettably I burst her bubble when I didn't respond as positively to her generosity as I would have today. *So What* if she can't let go of her things. We still donate generously in plenty of ways, and she has an enormous heart when it comes to giving and doing when it doesn't necessarily involve her own personal prized possessions (she just happens to prize *all* of her possessions). This year, I will praise her for gathering whatever donations she can, genuinely recognizing what a true sacrifice this is for her.

Listening

Another one of my buttons is when someone's not listening to me, and my daughter sure walks through this minefield a lot. For example, I'll be in the car talking about The Plans, such as what we're going to be doing the following weekend. Her response has nothing to do with what I've been saying, as she stares out the window and comments on the sign on the side of the road. *She's not listening to me! She doesn't care about what I'm saying!* I feel volcanic pressure building inside... gearing up to lash out at her for being so rude and inconsiderate and not caring enough about all I do for her... STOP. *So What* if she's not listening. It's not really important right now that she does. Her behavior in this moment has nothing to do with being rude or inconsiderate and it's not a measure of how much she cares or how interesting a human being I am. She's not listening because she's not interested in what's going on in the future, she's content right now being in the present. More power to her! There is no reason she needs to hear what we're planning weeks from now. If I'm looking for a way to make conversation, I'd better try another channel because this one's got no reception.

I'd love to say that *So What* works this neatly in every situation where she's not listening, but of course, that's far from true. Take the other night for example. I thought I'd made it crystal clear what I needed from her in order to get through the evening chaos. But at the end of the night when Bedtime arrived, there she was doing her own thing instead of doing what I direly needed her to do, and there I was blowing my top. The Listening and Procrastination buttons collided with the Bedtime hook, and oh, my, what an ugly scene ensued. It was a Perfect Storm scenario: When two or more buttons and hooks collide, the flames of red can completely blot out the words *So What.* All the marvelous talk that I'll get into later about embracing imperfection and forgiving myself went down the toilet along with my self-esteem. But we survived it, and before we went to bed we hugged and forgave each other. And the next morning I started anew looking for opportunities to practice *So What.*

Procrastination

My daughter usually has one speed: Fast. I used to joke that as a toddler she skipped learning how to walk, and went straight to running. But it never fails, when we're in a rush and it's time to get out the door, my runner switches to slow motion. Get your shoes! Where's your backpack? What do you mean you were supposed to bring back a signed form to school today? *WHAT* form?

Procrastination triggers other buttons related to needing to be on time and needing to keep to a schedule (discussed in later chapter on CONTROL). When we're finally in the car and I'm about to start the engine, it's time to pause. *So What* if we're a few minutes late. *So What* if it throws off my schedule by a few minutes. *So What*. What's more important right now is that I let go of the pent up stress and frustration so I can drive safely to school. And, by letting go and lightening up, together we'll be able to get on a fresh track to having a good day.

Television

Those who know me best would probably agree that my biggest button of all is The Television.

I recently read in what I consider to be a reputable source, that by the time the "average" American reaches 65, that person will have spent nine years of his or her life in front of the television. To many people, this in itself is probably *So What*. To me, it strikes a deep chord of grief and powerlessness. I want so badly for my daughter to choose books over television, or at least to make smart choices in her TV viewing. But alas, media and marketing genius have taken over her soul along with millions of other children, and I'm stuck listening to the irritating voice of Sponge Bob crashing in from the TV room. (Yes, despite the threat of becoming a social outcast, I confess that Sponge Bob is another one of my buttons.) But at least we both like Phineas and Ferb. So, we compromise.

So What if she's watching television more than just an hour a day as my parents enforced with me. *So What* if it's occasionally brainless entertainment vs. educational (like I didn't watch any brainless television when I was a child?). This is 21st century America. "All the kids are watching it." And you know what? There's something to be said for that being a little bit okay. They're not all jumping off the bridge with her following. They're watching Sponge Bob and she is, too. *So What.* I still generally enforce homework before television, and often enough she rides her bike around the neighborhood instead of being a couch potato in her spare time. *So What.* She's still on the way to developing into a lovely, caring, responsible woman, and I'm going to walk alongside her the entire way, supporting who she is, and doing a whole lot of *So What* to get myself past the areas where our personalities and preferences differ.

An interesting thing happened the other day. It started when my daughter didn't turn off the television at the end of her program as we'd agreed. I stormed into the room and angrily snapped off the power, which reduced her to a puddle of tears – primarily because she'd already gotten hooked into the next program and I'd cut her off from her fix. Then I had an epiphany: I was not angry at her, I was angry at the television producers. How insidious of them to suck children into this addictive zombie state, leaving the parents to be Evil Enemy Number One when it's time to cut them off. And here's how they do it: There is no break in the programming. They've perfected their style to ensure that one show runs straight into the next. No longer do they have commercials between shows, which marks a clear delineation between the end of one and the start of the next. Those savvy folks have learned to place their 5-minute commercial break BEFORE the end of the show, come back to a 30-second ending (or laugh spot as my daughter calls it), then ZOOM right into the hook of the opening of the next show.

Now, some of you may be laughing or rolling your eyes at me for not realizing this sooner, as it's probably been going on for ages. But the thing is, over the past dozen years or so I pretty much stopped watching television, and nowadays only watch it at times with my daughter (or listen from another room where I can tune in and tune out simultaneously). It wasn't until the battles and threats started escalating to ridiculous proportions (the finale was threatening to call the television company the next day to cancel service) that I finally had the "Duh" moment that I referred to previously as an epiphany. I wasn't battling with my daughter. I was battling with an addiction.

Once this truth came to light, my mind freed up to choose another path of intervention. I started by explaining to her that I wasn't angry with *her*, I was angry at the situation. I then began educating her about television programming, and how the people behind the scenes manipulate the audience into watching the next show and the next and the next. Then, together we found a strategy to learn how to beat them at the game. Now, when she gets sucked in, we have new language to use to break out of the cycle, such as, "There they go again!" We're no longer engaged in battle against each other, but instead have teamed up on the same side battling a common enemy. This is the kind of creative problem-solving that has become a lifesaver for our relationship and for my sanity.

This is also an example where pausing to evaluate *So What* comes out on the side of taking action, not letting go. I feel so strongly about the negative impact of television when not managed in moderation, I cannot imagine myself ever completely surrendering to it. However, note the keyword "moderation". I surrendered to the fact that Hannah Montana had become a household name, and through that surrendering enjoyed some fun moments of singing the show's theme song with my daughter. But I will not surrender to that television taking total control of my home. Understand that I am not dictating this as a rule for others to abide by. I'm merely providing an example of how respecting our own personal values helps identify those particular conflicts where there's less room for negotiation.

I confess, the way life goes, I end up relying on TV as the babysitter more often than I would like to admit. There are times when I'm exhausted, it's been a long day, we've been sweating it out over homework for awhile, I still need to finish doing the dishes or making dinner or whatever it may be, and… there's the television, and there she is asking to watch more of it. I'm faced with the choice of saying No Because I Already Set

Down The Rules For A School Night, or evaluating in the moment with *So What* if she watches one of her shows.

Oh, no! How awful to go against The Rules and to be Inconsistent! She'll never respect your words and your No again! Um, wrong again, inner nag. Parenting books often tout the importance of being consistent, and it's certainly true... to an extent. But the need for consistency should not preclude still being a thinking person and making a decision relative to what's happening now, as compared to the conditions that prevailed at the time of the initial decision. I've found that the more flexible I can be in regards to evaluating her requests as they come instead of rigidly abiding to pre-set rules, the more respect and cooperation I receive in return. I don't set rigid rules. I set guidelines. Sometimes, they're open for negotiation. And that works really well for us.

Instant Messaging and Instant Gratification

When I was my daughter's age, my parents only had to manage how much time I spent watching television and talking on the phone (which still had a cord so there were limited options as to where I could take my conversation). Now, in addition to television and the phone, there's the Internet, email, IM, chat rooms, video chat, social networking websites, texting, FaceTime, mass quantity apps and games to download to the cell phone or laptop or iPad...

Future generations of stressed out parents reading this book are going to LOL (translation for non-techies: Laugh-Out-Loud) at some of these references to "modern day" technologies such as cell phones and laptops, FaceTime and iPads. Who knows what's going to be the latest thing generations from now. Instead of texting, kids will be hopping over to a friend's house via holograms and astral-projection! (Can you imagine trying to enforce a curfew on astral-projection?) The point is, no matter what the technology and innovation of the day happens to be, there will always be new challenges to address. Some of the content within the pages of this book may become out-dated, but the fundamental principles behind *So What* are timeless.

With increasing performance of high-speed technology, everything's expected to be instant these days. We expect an answer to any question we search on the Internet within 2-3 seconds. We expect to get a response to a text message or IM immediately. A minute is too long to wait, unacceptable. This 21st century world of instant messaging and instant gratification (IMIG) is impacting our kids (and us parents) in a variety of ways.

In this IMIG culture, kids feel a pressing need to have everything NOW. As a parent, if I don't recognize this as a hook, my daughter's insistence to have everything NOW triggers my own urgency to act NOW. I get caught up in needing to make a decision NOW, needing to make a call NOW. Mom, I need a play date with a friend, text her mom NOW. Whoa, slow down! Whatever happened to sleep on it? Or at least wait a few minutes until we get home? *So What* if the call isn't made immediately. Her urgent "need" doesn't have to automatically translate to mine. Allowing a *So What* delay is an opportunity for us both to cultivate that thing called patience, which is currently at risk of becoming an endangered species.

Another fallout of IMIG is that it's become exceedingly easy to avoid meaningful interpersonal dialog. My sister told me a story about a party she attended recently, where several teenagers were on couches facing each other, silently texting. She asked one of the teens who it was he was texting, and he was texting someone *at the party*. Instead of walking across the room and engaging in a face-to-face conversation, he was content – even preferred – to just tap out cryptic messages to a virtual person on a keypad.

IMIG technology has shrunk both time and depth. Left to their own devices, our kids don't have to work to communicate, to get in touch with people, to have in-depth relationships, to gain knowledge by navigating their way through a public library... they can just hook up to their IMIG machines and deal with whatever is available to them that instant. To counter this, I make sure to have frequent face-to-face (or front-seat-to-back-seat) conversations with my daughter, not allowing the relationship to slip into cyber-land. Sure, there are times I let go with *So What* when my daughter is engaged in moderation with her electronics, such as playing with harmless apps on my iPhone. But there are other times when a *So What* evaluation will result in setting limits when I feel strongly that they're needed, such as no way allowing her to sign on to a social network at this time in her life. Luckily I still have a couple more years to cram as much cyber-safety into her brain as it can absorb, but this is certain to become a hot topic for us as she arrives at her teens. No doubt I'll be revisiting this subject in my sequel!

3.

Learning to Just Say Yes

One thing that's maddening and exhausting is the constant daily battle over No. It's a parent's job to set boundaries, and it's a child's job to push them as far as they can. The exchange is like a dripping faucet: it starts as just background noise, but after a few hours each small drop becomes deafening.

One morning while sitting in a waiting room, I read an article written by a mom who was at her wit's end battling her young daughter over every little thing all day long. She said a friend challenged her to spend one whole day saying Yes to everything her daughter asked of her. She reluctantly took the challenge and had quite a time of it, but at the end of that day realized there was a lot of value in simply saying Yes. I took this to heart and started noticing for myself how often I engaged in battles with my daughter just because I automatically said No versus inserting Yes instead.

Take a day and count how many times you say No, and notice how spent your energy is by the end of the day. Then, take the challenge and spend a day saying Yes! You'll likely experience for yourself the remarkable increase in energy and elevation of mood by day's end (if you can manage the initial stress of Letting Go, to be addressed later).

Of course, we can't live by Yes alone, but we can learn how to say Yes more often. A big part of *So What* is practicing just this – consciously choosing opportunities to say Yes instead of reflexively saying No.

Although there are many benefits to saying Yes, it's essential to first evaluate your motives.

Wrong reasons to say Yes

* Guilt

* Fear of causing disappointment

It's end of the day Friday after a particularly grueling week at work, and I'm late as I pick up my daughter from child-care. She runs into my arms and gives me a great big hug, and then without skipping a beat asks me to take her to the mall to buy a toy she saw on TV. Ugh. I'm exhausted. It's a couple of weeks before the holidays. The answer is No.

There go the tears and here comes the guilt. *You've been neglecting her all week. If only you didn't have to work so hard to make ends meet. She's still reeling over the divorce you so selfishly put her through because you couldn't hold it together for her sake.* I start wavering... *So What.* Pause, deep breath, look inward... and... the answer is still No. My reasons are justified. I don't need to fight the mall and spend extra money I don't have out of irrational guilt. Instead I can go home, make dinner, and spend quality time with her over a deck of cards and a bowl of popcorn.

It drives me nuts when my daughter begs, especially when she puts on those big puppy dog eyes and the turned down lip that looks so darn cute. However, she knows that begging is the last way to get me to change my mind. So next she puts on her lawyer's hat and presents an argument. She has this great opening statement: "Let me finish saying everything I want to say before you say yes or no." I'm not sure where she got that from, but it's very effective in getting me to listen attentively, and sets up the pause for me to determine whether or not this is a *So What* opportunity.

Depending on the circumstances and my evaluation of the situation, sometimes it's *So What* and I agree to what she wants. But other times it's *So What,* and I don't. Sure it's painful to witness my daughter's unhappiness, but disappointment is part of life. She won't learn how to deal with it if I constantly rob her of the opportunity out of my own conflicting needs, instead of sticking with what I believe is truly the best decision. She can cry, she can be disappointed, and then she'll move on, she'll get over it. I'm sympathetic and express compassion toward her, because I understand how bad it feels to not get what we want. And then I remind her to focus on what she does have, not just on what she doesn't.

Good reasons to say Yes

* Provides opportunities to teach personal responsibility and life skills

* Results in greater compliance with No

We're all familiar with the saying, "choose your battle". *So What* takes that little pearl of wisdom to the next level, by seeking out opportunities to say Yes.

I was in the kitchen rushing to get dinner made, when my daughter wandered in asking if she could help. My reactive response was to say No, because I was so intent on getting through the task in an efficient and timely manner and without the added mess that would most certainly result in her involvement. But instead, deep breath, I said Yes. *So What* that it will take an extra 15 minutes to get dinner on the table. *So What* that it'll take me twice as long to clean up afterwards. The payoff was that we had a lovely and memorable shared experience, and maybe she even learned a new thing or two about cooking (albeit her favorite thing to do while she's helping is to sample every ingredient and make cool designs in the mixing bowl). Of course I kept a close eye out for the dangers of hot burners and pans, and of course I said No to the large carving knife (not yet, honey), but in this case the benefits of saying Yes far outweighed the risks.

Here's another example of a positive outcome from saying Yes, when at first I'd been leaning strongly toward No. It was 7:30 on a Sunday night in mid-September, and she wanted to go to the community pool. It was pretty cold outside (by California standards anyway), and the schedule I had in mind was shower time next, not pool time. I paused and considered her request, and in that pause remembered how much I loved swimming on summer nights when I was a kid. So instead of saying No with all the reasonable explanations such as it being too cold and too late for a school night, I said Yes. She jumped for joy (rather shocked I might add), and raced to her room to change into a bathing suit. We walked to the pool, she hopped in immediately as I positioned myself at a nearby table... and then no more than five minutes later she called out to me, "I want to get out. It's too cold." No problem. I walked over and wrapped a towel around her as she emerged from the water, and we briskly walked home. No problem getting her into a bath that night, she couldn't wait to immerse herself in the warm water. And the rest of the night went smooth as butter.

There's so much relief in surrendering. Stop fighting the constant battle of rowing upstream; put the paddle down sometimes and enjoy the peaceful sensation of just floating downstream.

My favorite example of saying Yes took place during our trip to New York City. By the final day of our vacation, we'd done nearly everything on the list except for a few stragglers. I asked my daughter, "What is the one last thing you really want to do, that if we leave without doing it, you'll feel bad that you missed?"

Her answer? Go back to the M&M store and buy a souvenir there that she'd fallen in love with. Now, let me backtrack a bit... it had been the end of our first day in NYC when we'd happened upon the M&M store. After having said Yes to so many other souvenirs throughout the day and feeling the pinch in my purse (not to mention the tsks and admonishments from the "others" in my head for spoiling her too much), I was determined at the time that this last request was getting a No. And it did. So now here we were, the last day of our vacation, and I'm faced with two personal challenges inherent within her reply. First, I'd already said No, and now here she was bringing it up again, putting me in a position to weigh the value of being "consistent". Second, if we went all the way back to the M&M store just to buy that last souvenir, it would use up the whole day and we wouldn't get to see the rest of the things on the list (were any that important to either of us, anyway?).

So, what did I do? You guessed it. I said Yes. *So What* if I said No before and now I was saying Yes. That was three days ago, I'm allowed to reverse my position, especially knowing that was the one thing left to make the vacation a perfect success in her eyes. And *So What* if I was spoiling her on this vacation by buying her so many gifts. We have a deal... she can be spoiled as long as she's not rotten (i.e., unappreciative and greedy). And she'd been living up to her side of the bargain. *So What* about what "others" will think. That's the LEAST compelling reason of all. So... that last day we had a great adventure riding the subways back to the M&M store. The souvenir she was so thrilled about only cost about $12, and that night we had a wonderful time playing with it (an M&M slot machine, of all things). I have no regrets whatsoever for having said Yes to her that last day, and she has no regrets of things missed out from her dream-come-true trip.

Look for those opportunities to say Yes! When I say Yes, my daughter becomes more efficient in life skills such as cooking and hammering nails. She learns to make judgment calls for herself regarding when to say Yes and when to say No. And, she's less resistant when I do say No, because she trusts that I evaluate her requests fairly.

We have fewer battles and a lot more fun, just because I'm learning how to Just Say Yes.

4.

When No Means No

As important as it is to learn how to say Yes more often, it's equally important to recognize when it's time to say No, and to stick with No regardless of the internal and external pressures that inevitably nip at your heels.

Saying No requires the same conscious evaluation of the situation as saying Yes. What's your motivation?

Wrong reasons to say No

* Because I said so

* Because I should

Neither of these "reasons" holds any water in the eyes of our children. They only serve to build walls and diminish respect, the exact opposite of what we're aiming to accomplish.

I generally avoid using the words "always" and "never" since they're so absolute and tend to invite controversy, but in this case I'm making an exception and going out on a limb to make this point: "Because I said so" is *never* the way to say No. "Because I said so" escalates to "Who's the Boss" lose-lose power struggles. Kids learn really fast really well that they really are the boss of themselves, and they may go to dangerous measures to prove it. When you find yourself log-jammed in a power struggle, pause, think it through, then provide a logical reason for your position. "Because it's what I need right now" is much more effective and respectful than "Because I said so."

Another trap we fall into is saying No because we think we "should" based on either The Rules (you know, the ones that are there because they've always been there), or because of real or imagined judgments of what others may think of our parenting. Children see right through these flawed excuses, and will be inclined to either push back harder or else learn to stop asking and resort to sneaking and lying. Bottom line is, the Golden Rule is the only Universal Rule to follow without question: treat your child as you would want to be treated yourself. Respect is not demanded; it's reciprocated. You certainly have a right to say No, but think it through honestly and respond respectfully.

Good reasons to say No

 * Personal ethics and values

 * Respect for our own needs and wants

I've been teaching my daughter about product marketing since she was about three years old. No, I'm not going to buy that brand of yogurt solely because it has a picture of Dora on it. It tastes the same as the other yogurt, but costs an extra dollar just because of that picture. No, I'm not going to hop on the Internet and buy what they're advertising on television, even though the guy in the commercial says you'll lose the opportunity if you don't act now. Marketing is everywhere, creating the illusion of a need that has to be filled NOW. This is not a unique phenomenon, it's been hooking children of all ages for generations, but modern technology and finely tuned strategies have made it that much more powerful and compelling. I say No to buying on marketing-generated impulse, and I provide an explanation and education about it each time.

As much as I relished saying Yes to my daughter on our New York adventure, there was one time in particular when No was non-negotiable. We were exploring Central Park, and came upon a magnificent huge rock formation abuzz with children. My daughter gleefully hurried off to join in the fun, and normally I would have given an enthusiastic thumbs-up. However, I quickly realized that this time was different. It had only been six weeks since my spinal surgery, and I physically could not keep up with her. As much as I wanted her to enjoy herself and regretted having to deflate her elation, I had to say No. This was Central Park in NYC. There was no way I was going to say Yes and allow her to climb and venture anywhere she wanted, while I was unable to climb with her or to walk quickly enough around the wide perimeter to keep an eye on her. Although she was unhappy about the restriction, there was no argument – she understood my logic and there was no further discussion. As luck would have it, just a short distance away we discovered another place for her to climb and roam, and this time there was a bench where I could sit and still have full visibility of her whereabouts.

Sometimes a situation starts with a Yes, but then it's time to pull in the reigns. One evening I had done a *So What* over the television and allowed her to have it on longer than initially agreed upon. But after a while it started grating on me, and I just couldn't stand to have it on any longer. We needed to revisit our agreement, and we did. I shared with her that this was purely about me: I get irritable having the television on too much of the time as background noise. We share space, like roommates. If one of us is unhappy or uncomfortable in our living situation, then we need to talk about it and compromise. I'm kind of embarrassed to admit it, but this was a new thing for me, feeling justified in factoring my own personal needs and wants into the equation. To my pleasant surprise, there was no resistance from her. She respected my need and appreciated my honesty, and turned off the television with no fanfare.

Staying sane requires learning how to say No in other areas of our lives as well, such as taking care not to over-book ourselves. It's about prioritization, but it's not so clear-cut when everything feels like a priority. A good example is volunteering at school. It's important to me to be involved in my daughter's school, and the school direly needs parent volunteers. However, I have to know my limits and say No sometimes, or else volunteer work could easily turn into a third full-time job!

There are other areas where I've had to let go and say No as well. For example, I have finally surrendered to the fact that I simply cannot keep up with sending all those birthday cards and thank-you notes anymore. Sadly, I've also had to cut back on personal phone calls, letters, emails and invitations. There are just so many hours in the day and days in the week, and the stress of keeping up was outweighing the pleasure. It's not merely about curtailing these activities – the more significant test has been letting go of the irrational guilt involved with not being able to be all things to all people.

Rescuers become Victims

Saying No can be especially difficult when it comes to wanting to help someone out or to simply please. But saying Yes when we really need to say No can end up with a much worse outcome than if we'd said No in the first place.

Back in graduate school I learned about the Karpman Triangle, a psychological drama where individuals get hooked into a self-defeating dance of rescuer-persecutor-victim roles. Here's how the drama unfolds: The curtain opens on a perceived Victim, someone who appears to need our help. We step in to help, but if we don't set good boundaries and exert too much time and energy at the expense of our own needs, we fall into the Rescuer role. We know we've crossed the line between helping and rescuing when we start resenting the very person we were initially trying to help. This resentment is a sign that the Persecutor is about to enter the stage, either played by ourselves by getting angry at the Victim we no longer have much compassion for, or played by the Victim who turns on us for having over-stepped our bounds. Next thing we know, we've landed in the Victim role ourselves, dumped on and depleted of time and energy, with the tag line, "I was only trying to help".

In a previous story I described how I converted my Yes to a No in regards to my daughter's television viewing. This is an example of how I could have slipped into the Victim role had I not set the boundary when I did. She wanted to watch an extra hour of television, and I said Yes. But soon into that hour I realized I was starting to get very angry and irritable. Knowing about the R-P-V triangle, I quickly realized that my anger/resentment was a sign that I had not set a necessary boundary for myself. I really needed that television to be turned off. I could not just walk away from the sound, because our house is small and I could hear it from any of the rooms. Having identified this for myself, I was able to go talk to my daughter about it and work it out reasonably. Had I not been aware of the triangle, I likely would've stepped further into it by becoming the Persecutor and directing my anger toward her, or just slipping into the "poor me" Victim role and feeling perfectly miserable for the next hour and beyond.

Stated simply, we suffer the consequences when we over-step the bounds of saying Yes, and we need to recognize when it's time to set a boundary by saying No. It's not easy when we've become accustomed to the role of giving and doing for others, or when we feel guilt for wanting to place our own needs above someone else's. However, it's crucial to recognize and accept that Self-respect and Self-preservation are perfectly valid reasons to say No.

Promises vs. Intentions

Like many children, my daughter has the habit of interjecting "Promise?" whenever we're talking about future possibilities. It's so hard to say No and dash the flow of enthusiasm in the moment, but I'm very cautious about saying Yes to promises.

I only make a promise when I know I can keep it, and thus promises come sparingly. I've made a big point with my daughter to explain the difference between a promise and an intention. I will only make a promise when I have greater than 90% control over the outcome. Otherwise, it's an intention. Obviously, the 90% measure is figuratively speaking, but my point is that I try very hard not to make promises I may not be able to keep, and I think very carefully before saying Yes. For example, when it was time for her flu shot, while trying to calm her anxiety I said that it wouldn't hurt much and would be over in the blink of an eye. She immediately replied, "Promise?" Sadly, I had to say No, and explained that I couldn't promise something I had no control over. She didn't like that answer, but I believe she respected it.

Another example of a promise vs. an intention occurred recently in regards to our traditional Thursday pizza night. It was Tuesday and I didn't have any of her pizzas in the freezer. I mentioned this to her and she wanted me to promise to buy one in time for Thursday. I ran a mental check of my calendar for the next two days and could not see how I would be able to fit in a trip to the market (it's a special kind of pizza found only in a particular market across town). So I said No, I could not make that promise, but I did make it an intention. Then the conversation turned to roller-skating on Friday. Now, this one I was able to say Yes to a promise. I had already taken the day off work and confirmed hours with the roller-skating rink, so I stated confidently that Yes, roller-skating on Friday was a date and a promise, and she knows I keep my promises.

We all know that keeping promises is the key to building trust. But often we're compelled to make promises because we want so desperately to please our children, or to make up for the guilt we're feeling when the pressures of work and daily life lead us to feel like we're not giving them the attention they need. Be careful, don't let your guilt backfire on you and make things worse... make few promises, but keep the ones you make.

Oh, and about that pizza night... Thursday afternoon rolled around and I still hadn't made it to the store. My brain was racing in circles and my stomach was in a knot as I tried to figure out how I was going to manage it in the remaining time left... and you know what? *So What.* I finally surrendered and decided a trip to the market was something that just had to drop off my list, and that gets to be okay. I knew my daughter would be disappointed, but that's okay, too. She gets to be disappointed, she gets to express her disappointment – I was disappointed, too! I would love to have been able to get her pizza for her, but it just didn't work out this time. And that gets to be as far as it goes. I did not break a promise, I did not breach trust, we can share in the disappointment and then it's time to move on and fix something else for dinner.

We still went roller-skating on Friday.

Decide Not to Decide

Sometimes a situation presents itself where we're torn between Yes and No for equally valid reasons, as if our head and heart are split. The pressure rises internally (and potentially externally) to decide, but we just don't feel comfortable with either of the alternatives and need more information or clarity. Yes or No? No or Yes? Wait! There's a third option available: We can decide not to decide. *So What* if we don't make a decision instantly. What awful thing will happen if we don't? Unless the answer is something truly, validly awful, then we can decide not to decide... and sleep on it.

The suggestion to "sleep on it" has multiple meanings. For one, it can be simply a figure of speech for just taking a bit more time to work it out. Maybe a good night's sleep will help us to have a fresh perspective in the morning. On another level, we often literally do work things out in our dreams at night, regardless if we remember our dreams in the morning or not. That sense of magically having an answer to a problem when we wake up in the morning is indicative of this problem-solving function of dreams.

When we sleep on it and still wake up split down the middle, here's a tip that has proven to be very helpful when we still have another day or two to make a decision. Whatever the question at hand, begin by choosing Yes – privately – for purposes of this exercise only. Don't tell anyone this "decision" yet, just try it on for a day and then sleep on it again. The next day, choose No – privately – and imagine living with this alternative decision for the day. Usually, after trying on each decision, it's clear that one feels more right than the other.

If after all of this you still can't decide, then maybe there's another option out there that hasn't yet been identified. Imagine Yes is 1 and No is 10... search a little longer through the numbers 2 through 9. In the end, if nothing seems to work and you still feel hopelessly stuck, then just take a deep breath and choose the option you believe you can best live with. Don't get hung up on what's the Right decision to make, as if it's written in the sky somewhere and your job is to discover it. Decide that whatever decision you make *is* the Right decision, as simple as that. And don't trip yourself up by re-thinking your decision later if the outcome wasn't as desirable as you'd hoped, or beat yourself up with regret for not having chosen differently. Regret is based on the illusion of what might have been; there are no guarantees that the other path would've led to anything better than this one. Just look for a constructive lesson to take away from the situation and move on. Plenty more decisions await you; don't lose any more sleep over this one.

5.

Taming the Control Freak

I have the best job in the world for a single mom. My employer recognizes the importance of family and allows me the flexibility to work from home a few days each week. This affords me the luxury of taking my daughter to school every morning, picking her up on the days I'm not in the office, and volunteering to read in her classroom periodically. (I'm incredibly fortunate that she still wants me around that much, and I want to milk it for all it's worth before the day comes when she wants to put a 10-foot pole between us.)

As wonderful a setup as this is, the down side is that I'm constantly on duty from dawn to drop. From the time my alarm goes off at 6 a.m. until I finally pass out around 1 a.m., I'm going non-stop. A typical day of the week (which will sound familiar to many of you, just plug in your own particulars): Wake up, get myself showered and dressed, log on and attend to any fires that may be brewing at work, get my daughter up, pack a lunch if there's nothing she can eat on the school lunch menu, feed the cats, clean the litter box, check on my daughter again to make sure she's getting up and dressed, get something healthy in her for breakfast, check the laptop one last time before shutting it down and loading it along with everything else into the car, find my daughter's brush so she can brush her hair on the way, drive her to school, walk her to her line, kiss good-bye then back to the car, set up the phone with the headset and dial into my first meeting of the day as I drive to the office, do the work thing for several hours, pick up my daughter from her after-school care, get to an activity or maybe it's back-to-school night, figure out dinner, help with homework, get her bath or shower going, catch up with dishes and laundry while she's bathing, spend reading time with her before bed, sing her to sleep, finish dishes and straighten up the house a bit... and if I have any energy left, log back onto my computer to catch up with whatever work I missed out on while I was away.

Truth is, even when I was married, this was pretty much my same daily routine, which is a big part of where the asterisk in the sub-title comes into play. It's not just single moms dealing with this kind of crazy existence. My sister is neither married nor with children, but often her daily life is as crazy as mine, juggling her private tutoring business with a second job to make ends meet, tending to her home and personal care and relationship – all the stuff of life that each of us deals with to stay afloat.

With so much constantly going on, every hour of every day requires precision planning in order to maintain Control. What happens when a wrench is thrown into the plans, as inevitably occurs? Which is essentially what life is all about, wrench after wrench, or more positively reframed, surprise after surprise. That's when the Control Freak starts surfacing.

***Life is what happens to you while you're busy making other plans** – John Lennon*

I had an especially hectic day ahead, and in order to get through it, everything must work like clockwork – get my daughter to school, get to work in time for an array of meetings, pick her and her friend up after school, get her friend home in time to get to the swim lesson, and so on. The plan got as far as getting my daughter to school, and then came the awful sound in my car engine. So... instead of taking a right turn onto the freeway, I took a left turn into the auto shop. It was serious. I was told I had to leave the car and wait for a rental.

I had a choice here. I could panic and stress and brew and blame the world and myself for my misfortune. Or, I could apply *So What.*

Instead of beating myself up for not having had the forethought to bring my iPad with me (as if I'm supposed to have precognitive powers), and sitting it out in the cramped waiting room of the rental car agency (surrounded by other stressed out customers, mindless TV and embalmed pastries), I took a walk to a local coffee house and pondered more about *So What* as I sipped on a mocha latte and savored a croissant. By the time I got the call that my rental car was ready, my entire attitude had shifted, and I had a smile on my face instead of a growl. *So What* that I missed the conference call that morning. Nothing earth-shaking happened without me there, I'll catch up when I get back to the office. *So What* that I have another unexpected bill to pay. A year from now it'll all be completely irrelevant. I am alive another day. It's a good day.

No blame, no self-condemnation. Search for the positive, reframe: Thank goodness I followed my intuition and took the car in right then instead of waiting, or I could've blown out the whole engine. Thank goodness it didn't break down sooner, and I was able to get my daughter to school safely. Thank goodness I have the means to have a car in the first place. Thank goodness I have a secure job and supportive manager. So many things to be grateful for, yet how easy it is to take the one bad thing and play it over and over in our minds until we think the bad outweighs the good. The mind is a powerful thing.

We may not have control over the events in our lives, but we can *take control over the way we view them.*

Throughout the day I continued to get myself centered with this enthusiastic self-talk. By the time I picked up my daughter, I had a fine attitude and could enjoy hearing about her day, instead of bringing my self-inflicted angst into her world and blowing her day along with mine.

Letting Go of the Outcome

Spinning out of control leads to the need to grab more firmly onto control, or, rather, the illusion of control. Those times when I'm trying hardest to hold onto control are the times I most need to release my tight grip.

Letting go of the outcome can actually lead to the best one.

Only when we let go of trying to control all outcomes can new possibilities occur. A dramatic example of this for me was when I finally made the decision to divorce my husband. For years I had tried to control the outcome toward a happily-ever-after conclusion, to no avail. Finally, depressed and defeated, I knew I had to take a hard look at the alternative. But try as I might, I could not come up with a plan for what would come next if I were to decide to separate. Too many variables were uncertain and beyond my control. Yet I desperately needed to fully map it out for the sake of my daughter. How could I put her at risk by not knowing exactly how her future would unfold?

Finally, I could delay the inevitable no longer; it was time to take the plunge. Without knowing *for sure* what would come next, I had to take the first step and trust the rest to follow. And it did. By letting go of trying to control the uncontrollable, my path unfolded in seemingly miraculous ways. The house sold quickly, the perfect next home presented itself in nearly perfect synchronization (albeit a few weeks span in between, but even the interim hotel accommodations fell right into place), my daughter didn't have to change schools so she could at least have some stability during the major transition, and the multitude of other details large and small all managed to come together by just allowing them to unfold one segment at a time.

When we're stuck in the mode of needing to control all outcomes, we're limited to only the outcomes that we can imagine. Most of the time, it's the very outcomes we *cannot* imagine that are actually the ones that turn out to be the best. It's only by letting go that these unimaginable outcomes can manifest.

With a decision of this magnitude, it may be hard to fathom employing the words *So What.* And yet, this is precisely the mind-set required in order to break through an impasse such as this. *So What* if I don't have every single angle covered. Yes, this means there's some risk involved, but *So What?* Why do we so often regard risk as something to be avoided? There are times in our lives when fundamental change is necessary, and the only way to achieve this level of profound change is to risk venturing into unfamiliar territory. If all we ever choose is the known, then we can never truly achieve core change inherent only in the unknown.

Bracing for the Fall

I vividly remember the moment I was told that I could take my newborn baby home from the hospital. Gazing intently at this delicate little seven-pound being, I was suddenly in complete awe of the responsibility I had just taken on. Eight years later, I'm still just as keenly aware of the responsibility, but what constitutes "responsibility" has multiplied exponentially in complexity.

It's essential to find the balance between allowing my daughter her independence to make choices and learn from natural consequences, versus when it's time for me to step in for education and safety's sake. Left to my own devices, I'd be directing her every step in order to guard her from the multitude of mines in the loaded field of life. Fortunately for my daughter, I'm conscious enough of my controlling tendencies to avoid impulsively acting on them.

I pride myself in being the Efficiency Expert (a gentler term for Control Freak). Every thought is about the most efficient way to get from point A to point B. If I have five destinations to hit, I'm planning the most efficient route. Even when I'm checking out at the grocery store, I'm placing my goods on the belt in an order that will be most efficient to bag them. This is my lifeline, this is what allows me to manage a job (where, by the way, planning is a key part of my job description) and parenthood and everything else involved in this crazy life I lead. So of course when my daughter says she wants to do it her own way or has some idea that's not part of the plan, I have to take a deep breath and remind myself what's most important in this moment.

The planner has the ability to see many outcomes all at once. So often I want to just stop her in her tracks, to protect her. But no, she must have ample leash to explore and discover cause and effect on her own. It's a constant challenge to find the balance between these two polarities, a middle ground where I'm protecting without over-protecting. I need to step to the side and allow her to make her own decisions, to learn her own way, and to gain strength in her ability to survive the outcome.

Although my own anxiety rises when I fear she's headed for pain and heartache, I must keep my eye on the target: open communication and trust. I can voice an opinion and offer suggestions, and then I need to let go and be supportive of her own process. What's most important is that at the end of the day, she can turn to me with her tears and disappointment, as well as with her pride and joy. No matter what the outcome, there's no place for "I told you so."

So What is a daily exercise in creative parenting. It requires weighing all the variables in the moment: What's important to her, what's important to me, what does this one particular outcome really matter in the larger scheme. It's a minute-by-minute, day-by-day practice of discernment regarding what's so important that I have to intervene and take control, vs. when I can say *So What* and allow for the natural evolution of this fabulous young person who is my child.

It's a scary world, I have limited control, but trying to grab harder onto the illusion of control is not the solution to protecting her. As much as I want to shield her from harm and ease her way, this simple fact exists: I can't always be there to catch her when she falls, but I can and will be there afterward to comfort her and help her back up on her feet.

6.

Let It Be

As a kid, I hated it when my mom would go on and on with her lecturing. I'm sure her honorable intent was to better me as a person, but unfortunately it had the opposite effect of making me feel small, stupid and ashamed. And I doubt I ever got whatever the core message was that she was trying to deliver.

Imagine my embarrassment when I catch myself doing the same thing to my own child!

So, lecturing is out, but that's easier said than done. In order to stop myself from stepping into that trap, I need to stop feeling so compelled to turn everything into a lesson, and especially to stop drilling it in.

Enter these truly simple words of wisdom and a great complement to *So What*:

Let it be.

Find the positive instead of focusing on the negative, and appreciate what is instead of slipping into the fear of what might have been.

The first couple of weeks after my neck surgery, I spent a good deal of time in bed. Family flew into town to help out the first week, but by the second week it was pretty much just my daughter and me, with considerate friends dropping by in the evenings. One morning my daughter appeared at my bedside saying, "I brought you your coffee Mama." I froze inside. My immediate internal response was to freak at the thought of her spilling it all the way up the stairs (how could I clean it up in this state?) or the "what if" she had burned herself (silly, of course – it didn't happen, so why fret about it after the fact?). But instead of voicing any of these fear-ridden thoughts, I took a deep *So What* breath and genuinely thanked her for her thoughtfulness. She felt so proud, and I was so glad to have squelched my initial impulse to warn her off ever doing it again (which would have served no purpose other than to negate the positive).

Then there was the infamous height chart. One day she asked if she could pencil a height chart on the wall of our new home. Sure, why not. It was a tradition in our other house to put little slash marks and dates on the doorframe like lots of families do, no big deal. A few minutes later she cheerily dragged me out of my room to show me her proud accomplishment. Imagine my surprise when I saw that she'd drawn a foot-long picture of a girl in the middle of the entry hall, her plan being to make the hair grow taller as she grew! My internal knee-jerk reaction was to reprimand her and expound on the evils of defacing a wall, but luckily I caught myself with the *So What* mantra. Instead, I complimented her on her creativity and took a picture of it to always remember the moment. She was so pleased with herself, and I'm not in any hurry to paint over it. I don't care what other people may think when they see it – the imaginary "other people" that would judge me harshly for being too lenient with my daughter. *So What.* I'm proud of myself for resisting the lecture and being able to let it be, and I love walking past this precious work of art every day.

Another poignant example where I was able to let it be was an incident that occurred at the beach. We'd been driving a long time and stopped at a popular beach where we could stretch our legs and hang out for a while. We were standing a short distance from the ocean, when in her excitement she darted knee-deep into an approaching wave. The fact that she was wearing new shoes and long pants and that both the air and the water were only about 50 degrees didn't occur to her until after her impulsive, exuberant act. My spur-of-the-moment reaction was to get angry with her for having demonstrated such poor judgment. But fortunately I came to my senses in time to recognize this was not the best approach to be taking here. She was just being a kid, and the natural consequences taught her everything she needed to know. She was freezing and miserable and upset, so instead of lecturing I comforted her and took care of her immediate need to get dry and warm. There was no need to obsessively drill in any lesson. *Let it be.* Once she was in a change of clothes (which we fortunately had in the car), we recovered with a delicious bowl of soup at a lovely outdoor café.

Along the same lines, asking "Why did you do that?" is such a pointless exercise, and generally has the same result as lecturing. Nine times out of ten you're going to get "I don't know" as an answer, and it's probably the honest truth. *So What.* She put foot lotion on her face. Why did you do that? I don't know. Instead of pressing it further and filling the void with a barrage of vacant words, *So What. Let it be.* It really doesn't matter, lecturing isn't going to achieve anything. Just help her wash it off.

Bedtime

Good parenting rule #456: your child, especially an eight-year-old, should be in bed by 8:30 p.m. Well, my kid is not an 8:30 p.m. go-to-bed kind of kid. Not even when she was a young child. Not that she would rebel when I did try to put her to bed at that time, but she still had so much excess energy she'd be climbing the walls (literally – she'd lay perpendicular to the wall with her feet walking up it). It was kind of pointless. Eventually it evolved to, let's see what her own natural rhythm is, her inner clock. Well, yikes, she may be only eight years old, but her bedtime clock is around 10 p.m. I told that to a couple of parents recently and they blanched. Although they didn't speak the words, their faces clearly communicated that they were appalled that I would let my child stay up that late. But that's just the way it is. Her motor shuts down at 10 p.m. and revs back up every morning at 7 a.m., no alarm clock required. And that seems to be enough sleep for her. *So What* that this doesn't comply with some latest greatest parenting manual. *So What* that other parents may compare and judge. *Let it be.* My daughter is energetic, healthy and happy, and that's one less battle to deal with (or 365 less battles to deal with, if you look at the bigger picture).

Still, there are nights when her clock doesn't kick in even on this late-night schedule, and I start to get an edge. I check in with my motivation again: How much is about Bedtime Rules expectations, how much is about tending to her bodily needs (after all, the child does still need sleep), and how much is about my own need to get her situated so I can get back to work? When laid out this way, the answer is clearly a combination of addressing both her needs and mine. It's no longer a battle of wills, but instead is about creative problem solving. My clever daughter has provided the solution for this particular scenario. She'll say, "Work me to sleep, Mama." I bring my laptop over and stretch out next to her, allowing her to tap a few keys and help with whatever I'm doing. We engage in some quality day's end chatting, and within a few minutes her motor turns off. She's out like a light. No battles, sweet dreams. Sure, there's something to be said about it not necessarily being the same quality bedtime ritual as reading together or singing her to sleep, but *So What.*

Sometimes it's just going to be working her to sleep, and that's okay with us.

When Right is Wrong

It's not uncommon for my witty daughter to come up with a valid argument that persuades me to change my mind. She's right. But who's Right or Wrong doesn't really matter and misses the point – we're a team working together to find a mutually satisfying solution.

I would no sooner argue with my daughter about who's right or wrong than I would with my co-workers or subordinates at work. As manager and as parent, I carry the onus of responsibility and it's my job to set up processes and guidelines in order to run things as smoothly as possible, but in the end our success depends on us working together as a team. In my workplace, I don't achieve results by playing the role of dictator demanding respect for authority. I achieve results by demonstrating respect and building trust as we work together toward a common goal, and a by-product of this approach is the good fortune of earning their respect in return. With mutual respect, we can get far more done with far less stress. Parenting is no different.

Yes, in both roles I'm still in a position of authority when it comes to making a final decision, but it's not being driven by the need to be Right or to make the Right decision, as if what's "right" is written in some elusive rule book somewhere, or is the kingpin of my ego. Making effective decisions requires letting go of the need to be right. It's about considering all viewpoints and then trusting my experience and intuition to take the action that I deem to be most beneficial.

It's so pervasive, this need to prove who's more right. And it's no easy habit to rid ourselves of, as it becomes ingrained at such an early age. Recently I overheard another round of squabbling between my daughter and her BFF, as they once again got locked into a war of wills: Uh-uh! Uh-huh! Uh-uh! Uh-huh! I generally try to be invisible and not intervene, but this time I became impatient and finally blurted out: There's nothing to gain from arguing over who's right and who's wrong! *Let it be.* There's room for BOTH to be "right"... now how do we move forward from here?

After a moment of silence, the girls slipped back into the game they'd been playing prior to the standoff. And I graciously returned to donning my invisibility cloak.

7.

The Good-enough Factor

A few years ago, while driving to pick up my daughter from preschool, I heard an interview on the radio with Judith Warner, the author of *Perfect Madness: Motherhood in the Age of Anxiety.* I fought back tears as I listened to her describe the insanity I was living, trying desperately to keep up with expectations of the "perfect mom" that I was unwittingly buying into from others and piling on myself. And this was before the added weight of becoming a single mom! When I got home I rushed to buy the book online, but ironically never managed to make time to read more than the first chapter or so. Still, it sits prominently on the bookshelf in my bedroom, a constant reminder that I am not alone in my rebellious quest for sanity.

Unfortunately, instead of joining forces with and deriving strength from our fellow besieged motherfolk, we too often build defensive walls of judgment that conversely serve to keep us apart. We simultaneously fend off judgmental messages from our own mothers along with judgment from our peer mothers who are dealing with judgmental messages from their own mothers. What a psychologically messy lot we are, consciously and unconsciously passing judgment on ourselves, our sisters and our children for never being good enough. STOP THE MADNESS!

In order to relinquish our judgmentalism, we need to recognize it in the first place.

My mom was wholly determined to raise her children the Right way, to be as Perfect as we could be. What I know now that I didn't know then, is that she was just as hard or even harder on herself. Although she meant well, the bar was set so high that I felt I could never reach it, could never be good enough. I believe this was true for her as well, though in her lifetime she never stopped trying and never stopped pushing.

Instead of developing a competitive nature, I went down the compare-and-contrast track. I'd automatically compare myself to others with the result of either superficially raising myself up, or pushing myself down even lower than where I started, and I was much better at accomplishing the latter. Regrettably, either way only served to unconsciously reinforce this judgmental way of thinking.

Now, this never-good-enough script was not a new revelation. I'd been working on re-writing it for much of my adult life. But something about having a child of my own tripped me up and sent me backsliding. Although I had done a pretty good job of achieving good-enough status when I was on my own, suddenly I found myself direly missing the mark in the role of parent. Without realizing it, I had slipped right onto the path of the Perfect Parent Syndrome (more about this to come).

Having recognized the root of my descent, I was able to brush the dirt from my knees and get back on track.

I am good enough, as a person and as a parent.

The best part about letting go of internal and external judgment is that it allows me to appreciate my daughter purely for who she is, and to let go of fear of what she may or may not become. She is seen, is loved, is encouraged to be and discover her self. I'm doing my best to give her whatever guidance I can, and then get out of her way. So far, despite my bumbling, she is thriving and blossoming beautifully.

The Perfect Parent Syndrome

Perfect Parent Syndrome (PPS) begins even before the birth of our children. I attended a pre-natal parenting class where the instructor was talking about the benefits of breastfeeding. Well, I already knew that wasn't an option for me, being on the path of adoption. When that came up in discussion, oh the pitying looks I got! *Not even a bonafide mother yet, and already you're behind the curve!*

Then came daycare. The competition begins! Is your child in swim lessons yet? Is she signed up for soccer? Have you started using flashcards? As daycare morphed into preschool, the expectations became even more intense. Is she learning an instrument? Are you teaching her a second language? Has she taken the entrance exams for kindergarten? ENTRANCE EXAMS FOR KINDERGARTEN?! *Oh, my, you're not trying to get your child into the elite private elementary school that all the rest of the parents are trying to get their children into? Don't you care about your child's chances of getting into college?* (we're talking PRESCHOOL)

Private schools aside, navigating the public school system is a challenge in itself! There's the school in your district, then there are the magnet schools, the charter schools, the cross-district transfers, the inter-district transfers, the Better Schools websites with all the different categories of ratings... it's another full-time job just trying to figure out how to get your child into kindergarten and which school to choose. *What if you make the wrong choice? Your child could be doomed!*

And how about those birthday parties. Do we invite all the kids in the class, or dare we select only those who are friends (which potentially changes daily)? Is it okay to bypass the party gift bag if they're already going home with a bag of piñata candy? My house is a wreck, what will the other parents think? *How can they trust you with their children if you can't even take care of your own home?*

PPS madness was escalating out of control... until I finally latched onto *So What*. First of all, I discovered that most parents are *relieved* to see another house not in perfect condition! We're all in the same boat here, and a Perfect Presentation doesn't make me look good, it makes them feel bad. That's certainly how it is for me, anyway. When I pick up my daughter at a friend's house, if there are piles and clutter, I feel in good company. When I enter a spotless house, I feel inadequate. *So What* if my house isn't perfectly kept up. I've finally joined the club of Imperfect Parents, and I'm proud to be a member.

My *So What* perspective has gone a long way toward alleviating PPS school-related stress as well. An online chat group had formed for parents of children in my daughter's class. A couple of weeks into the new school year, some of the parents began expressing concern in the chat about the difficult homework assignments and general lack of communication and direction. Within just a couple of days, anxiety and frustration had really started to mount as more parents were joining into the discussion. One afternoon, while standing outside the school entrance waiting for our kids to emerge, a dad I'd become acquainted with asked me what I thought about the homework situation, clearly expecting me to jump on the bandwagon so he could elaborate more as well. But instead of jumping on, I responded from a genuine *So What* state of mind. Yes, my daughter was struggling with the homework as well, and some of the new class policies were a bit unclear to me, but... *So What*. It's just the first month into the school year, and it takes time to adjust to new things. She's responding well to her teacher and on the whole seems to be doing fine, so it's just not that big of a deal for me in this moment.

A few days later when we met again in the same spot, he thanked me for my input the other day. He said it really helped him gain a new perspective, and he was able to relax more about the whole homework issue after that. I was surprised and delighted to see the positive impact my simple demonstration of *So What* had made on this fellow parent.

School isn't just a challenge for our children. It's a tremendous daily challenge for us parents as well. The sanest way to get through it is by parents supporting parents. The more we can talk to one another and share our ideas in non-judgmental ways, the more we can come to the table with a centered, positive state of mind instead of contributing to a snowball effect of negativity and panic.

Divorce

Grief, Regret, Guilt, Shame - sorry remnants of my failed marriage and divorce, little gremlins that try to drag me back to the past instead of allowing me the pleasures of the present. I'm so good at beating myself up with What-if's and If-only's. On top of all the real-life day-to-day challenges, this pervasive internal shaming voice tries relentlessly to trip me up: *How awful and selfish of you to have put your daughter through divorce. How terrible it is for her to have to split time between two parents and households.*

Or is it?

It's not what I'd planned or what society condones (even though more than 50% of us have been there done that). But is it really that bad for my daughter? When I put on the internal earmuffs and try to view this as objectively as I can, I see that in many ways she's actually thriving better than ever before. She has a role model now of a mom who can be completely herself and self-sufficient, and we can be together in genuine, unique ways that were not accessible in the other configuration. When the gremlins start rattling off their doom and gloom messages, I dismiss them with *So What*, she's doing just fine. This is the 21st century where children grow up successfully in all kinds of families and living situations.

When I was growing up, the divorce rate wasn't what it is today. Children of divorce were in the minority and their seemingly dire family lives talked about in hushed tones. I imagined the same dreaded fate for my child, to be an outcast living in shame. Um, wrong. That was my own head-trip, and it was up to me to shake it off so I didn't lay it on her. Yes, there will be challenges for her as a child of divorce, such as going back and forth between households and adjusting to different sets of rules and expectations. But it will not be a stigma or stain on her beautiful being.

I have a choice in regards to how I'm going to view divorce, and in turn what attitudes I'm going to hand down to my daughter. *So What* that she'll be raised by a single mom now, time-sharing with her dad. That's just the way it is. Each of us grows up with a unique life story, some more elaborate than others, and now this is part of hers. Of course, *So What* does not imply that divorce is no big deal for a child. It's a huge deal, no argument there. The key value of a *So What* attitude here is in normalizing instead of catastrophizing the mere fact of divorce, freeing up mental and emotional resources to deal with all the subsequent variables involved.

Oddly enough, now that I wear the mark of divorce, when I'm out from under the self-inflicted shame that I'm so adept at laying on myself, I feel a great deal of relief and a lot less pressure to keep up the Perfect Parent Syndrome. I'm wearing it on my sleeve now: I Am Not A Perfect Parent With A Picture Perfect Marriage. I am imperfect. I am human. As my daughter would say, Yay Me!

Imperfection and Forgiveness

The main wisdom I've acquired in my eight years of parenting is to let go of my need to be "perfect." By lightening up on myself, I'm lightening up on my daughter as well.

As a kid, I'd bring home a report card with 5 A's and one B, and my mom would ask why I got the B. Never good enough unless it's 100%. This is ingrained in my personality, and I have to work hard to consciously respond differently with my daughter. She'll clean her room 80% and I'll see the 20% still messed. But good news: I must be doing something right, because she's the one now who calls me on it!

Who would've thought that by being an imperfect mom, I'm actually doing the best role-modeling ever – not just as a mom, but as a person. This *So What* deal is great, but of course it's imperfect just as I am. When I slip and lose my patience, when the "ugly face" comes out, afterward I apologize for my part in our altercation, and she apologizes for hers. Then we both say "I forgive you" and move on. I'm readily able to forgive others, but the greater challenge is forgiving myself. It comes much more easily for her than it does for me, but I'm learning. She is my teacher.

An area where letting go of perfectionism is particularly challenging is homework - for both of us. For her part, there are times when I'll point out a mistake, and she'll get very upset with herself. I remind her it's okay, that's what learning is all about, no need to get so upset when she doesn't instantly get something. This is a lesson I'm constantly taking to heart myself as well.

For my part, when I'm reviewing her writing assignments, the perfectionist in me is compelled to point out the various areas of improvement, but fortunately the kindly mom knows better. *So What* if she gets a B instead of an A. She's in 2nd grade. Lighten up! Will I be able to take the same approach when she's in high school? I certainly hope so. As long as she's putting forth effort, I'm proud of her achievements whatever they may be. If she asks for my help, I'm here to give it. I cannot single-mindedly lay my own hopes and expectations on her. I can put them out there, encourage her to consider them, and then the rest is up to her.

In a parent volunteer meeting at school this year, a young mother at one point blurted out, "Oh, I'm such a horrible parent!" It made me cringe. We are NOT horrible parents just because we're imperfect. We HAVE to work on that negative self-talk. Our children pick up on it, and take away that there's some elusive standard of perfection that they're supposed to achieve, and if they don't, there's something terrible about them. It's a setup. There's no such thing as perfection. Perfection is an illusion. Perfection is 100% subjective. What's "perfect" in one person's eyes is not the same in another person's eyes.

These statements about perfection are clichés. We've all heard them (or some version of them). Yet we stubbornly continue to make unrealistic demands on others and ourselves. Sadly, too often the outcome is to put someone else down in order to raise ourselves up. Our children discover this at such a young age, when someone in their class is different (AKA not perfect) and therefore becomes a target of ridicule and exclusion. They're trying themselves to be perfect so as to avoid the horrors of being the target. The perfect body, the perfect personality, the perfect clothes, the perfect mind, the whole popularity thing based on who's perfect enough to be in the In crowd. I practice *So What* psychology with my daughter as much as possible, but I'm fighting an uphill battle because the forces on the other side are so strong and pervasive. The more parents start embracing the *So What* attitude and jump on the good-enough bandwagon, the healthier our next generation will be.

The goal is not Perfection. The goal is Authenticity... with ourselves, and with our children.

The Replay Button

An unfortunate incident happens once. Then we play it over and over again in our minds, until our brain lodges the felt sense that it's happened a hundred times or that it "always" happens to us.

I lost my patience with my daughter one evening and said something unkind that I immediately regretted. Although I apologized right then and she accepted my apology, I still felt awful about it and kept running it through my head. By morning I had magnified the event to such an extent that I was certain I'd destroyed her self-esteem and made a huge, irreparable dent in our relationship. When I apologized again to her, she looked confused for a moment and then replied, "Oh, that? I'd forgotten all about it." End of discussion. I'd lost a night's sleep and slipped several rungs on the good-enough ladder, all because I let the replay button get the best of me.

Another example of the power of the replay button was when my daughter said to me after school one day, "No one wants to play with me." When I asked for specifics, I learned that a single child rejected her on the playground. This one rejection played over and over again in her mind eventually translated into "everyone" rejecting her, instead of seeing it for what it was, which was simply one child's rejection in one specific situation.

So What breaks these negative generalizations and keeps situations in perspective. *So What* that this person doesn't want to play with me today.

I'll find someone else to play with. Then hit the replay button and queue up some positive experiences instead of the negative!

Not Buying Into Bullying

Tragically, it's not always ourselves pressing the replay button. Bullying through incessant teasing and harassment is a very serious issue for our children. It's no longer confined to the playground or neighborhood; the 21st century has now introduced us to cyber-bullying that takes place through the many social network venues on the Internet.

Bullying takes many forms. In my daughter's case, it's been going on since preschool with various girlfriends hounding her with threats such as, "If you don't do this then you won't be my friend"... "You can't be friends with her if you want to be friends with me". On a daily basis I listen to her stories and try to get her to that *So What* place in herself. *So What* if that girl doesn't want you to be friends with the other. You're the boss of you, make your own choices, and if she decides your choice isn't good enough for her, then *So What*. She can find another friend.

It's not just the behavior of walking away from the person who is bullying; it's the healthy attitude that needs to come with it. Strengthening self-esteem with techniques such as *So What* is essential. *So What* if that kid thinks I'm a nerd, I like myself just the way I am. *So What* if they won't let me into their popular inner circle, there are plenty of other kids to make friends with.

As a parent, I may feel angry and want to jump to her rescue, but unless she's truly in danger, my intervening would only serve to rob her of the confidence that comes with handling it on her own. My role is to be someone she can trust to talk to about anything that's upsetting her. The more I release unrealistic expectations on myself to have all the answers and solutions and instead allow myself to just be a compassionate human being, the more approachable and trustworthy I become.

I AM GOOD ENOUGH.

I am Good Enough without having to prove I'm Better Than.

I am Good Enough even if I'm not As Good As.

I AM GOOD ENOUGH.

8.

Embracing Today

My daughter and I play this game when we're driving long distances (which to her may be five minutes). She says over and over, "Are we *there* yet?" and I repeat back, "No, but we're *here.*" It drives her nuts, but keeps me sane.

The original concept for this book was about moving from lost to found, the reclamation of my Self after transitioning from single to married to motherhood and ultimately to single motherhood. I kept putting it off, thinking I couldn't write it until I was already there (i.e., had finally reclaimed my long-lost Self). Finally, I took a stab at it, fooling myself into thinking that I was close enough to *there* to get started. The first draft bombed terribly, not only because I wasn't anywhere close to being *there*, but more importantly because I'd forgotten that there is no *there*. Once I was hit in the head with this Duh revelation, the inspiration for *So What* came to me. I'm writing it today even though I'm not *there*, because there is no *there*, there's only *here*.

Today, I'm practicing engaging in the world as me, letting go of self-condemnation and intolerance of my imperfection.

I am not a perfect mother. I am not a perfect person. I am just... me. And that is Good Enough. It seems to be good enough for my daughter, too, who is at a wonderful age where she still respects and admires me (hasn't yet hit tweens and teens). But most important, it's good enough for *me*. Or at least, I'm on my way to accepting that.

There is nothing more humbling than parenthood. I majored in child development in college, went on to get a masters degree and license in marriage, family and child counseling, read dozens of books, counseled numerous families... but regardless, my child and I still lock horns, I have my share of explosions, and a wealth of lessons come at me on a daily basis. While all that experience and education is no doubt a valuable part of what I bring to the parenting table, when I'm with my child, all that matters is being spontaneous, authentic and present.

When I'm in the *So What* zone, my relationship with my daughter deepens. I'm not so uptight and controlling; I'm more relaxed and able to let her have full leash to be who she is. Maybe now she will grow up with a healthy good-enough factor, be naturally loving and forgiving of herself and others. Believe at the core that she is loved and lovable. That's far more important than clean teeth.

Spontaneity

Plans are great – I couldn't function without them. But after the plans are made, be ready to set them aside and go with the flow.

My daughter was set on going to New York for our annual big adventure. I was a bit apprehensive about this, as I hadn't been to New York in many years and the idea of traipsing around this crowded, unfamiliar city with my young daughter evoked quite a bit of anxiety, to say the least. So I set about doing what I usually do at times like this: I started planning. First, I bought books about New York for Kids, and went online to check websites and pre-purchase tickets to the most sought-after attractions. A good friend of mine bought me a cool New York app for my cell phone, where I could build a daily itinerary complete with walking maps and GPS. I had every bit of that trip planned to every detail, yet on our first morning in the Big Apple, I asked her, "So, what would you like to do your first day here?" Without hesitation she said what her heart was most desiring: she wanted to go to the American Girl store. Was that what my app would've recommended? Was that the most efficient place to begin the day according to the itinerary? Not in the least. And we happily set off for American Girl store.

Spontaneity opens the door to new adventures and opportunities. It was a routine morning, I was at home planted in front of my computer totally stressed with work, when I decided to step away to get some distance and clear my head. It had been a few days since I checked my PO box across town, so I got in my car and headed over. Just as I was about to arrive at my destination, I realized I had forgotten my PO box key back home. Not happy. Now, instead of stress subsiding, it was increasing! A minute or two of expletives later (shouted aloud in the privacy of my own car), I impulsively turned my car into the driveway of a nearby shopping center, and was utterly shocked and thrilled to spot a dear colleague I hadn't seen in 20 years step out of one of the stores! I pulled my car into the first parking spot I could find, and caught up with him just as he was about to drive off. If the timing had been any different, our paths would not have met and we'd have missed the opportunity to reconnect. By the time I returned to my car, I had a whole new outlook for the day. *So What* that I'd driven all the way across town and had forgotten my PO box key. The trip had been far from wasted.

No Day But Today

I have this tendency to live each day as if I'm racing with time. *So What* are the words of surrendering to the present, to what is. I am no longer trying to control what another person does, thinks or feels. I am no longer trying to control all outcomes. How freeing it is! As soon as I say *So What*, both body and mind relax, and I get a glimpse into Now. And Now is where Peace, Joy and Gratitude reside.

An event occurs. It is our *interpretation* of that event that influences our subsequent feelings and actions. I can view life as unfair and hard, or I can choose to view life as an adventure. I can interpret my racing heart and sweaty palms as anxiety, or I can interpret those same bodily responses as excitement.

When someone I trust says something that hurts my feelings, I can feel bad, angry and rejected, or I can choose to believe that this person cares about me and wouldn't deliberately try to hurt me. Perhaps I misinterpreted their intentions. Instead of brewing silently on the negative, I can choose to be optimistic and talk about it.

Unhappiness is about being stuck in the past on what we can't undo; anxiety is about being fixated in the future on what hasn't even happened yet. The simple truth is, all that's real is the present; the rest is purely imagination and illusion. When I'm unhappy or anxious, I need to pause, take a deep breath, and then inventory my thoughts to determine where they've been dwelling. This simple act will bring me back to the present, and from here I can make a conscious decision about what I'm going to think and do next. We have far more control over our thoughts and emotions than we give ourselves credit for.

Being There

My daughter asked me at dinner one night, "Did you do what you always wanted to do in your life?" Wow, what a question. I was surprised and pleased with what came out of me: "I didn't really have something I always wanted to do... but when I was a camp counselor I loved doing that, so I became a family counselor and I loved doing that, and then I wanted to get into technology and I love doing that, and then I wanted to be a mom and I found you and I absolutely love doing this... so I guess the answer is Yes, I did do what I really wanted to do in my life. I've had a wonderful life."

So What that I didn't get to be a rock star. *So What* that I didn't get to live happily ever after with Prince Charming. Instead, look at all the things I *did* get to do. *So What* brings us back to the present and reminds us to choose gratitude for what is, instead of holding onto regrets for what might have been.

I have one chance to raise my child the way I sincerely believe is the best way possible. I have released myself to be a free thinker, and I want to teach my daughter the same.

Life isn't perfect. People aren't perfect. We're all just doing the best we can to navigate through the journey.

Are we there yet? No, but we're here. And here is a wonderful place to be.

9.

Going the Distance

Parenting is like running a marathon. A very long marathon, with no finish line. In order to survive and thrive, we have to condition and pace ourselves just like professional athletes. We need to take care of ourselves physically and mentally, and we require a support team helping to sustain us every stretch of the way. Most of all, we need a *Yes I Can* attitude, belief in ourselves that we can go the distance. It's grueling and it's awesome, and I'm not exaggerating when I say that at the end of each day, I utter words of gratitude for having made it around another lap. And if that particular day was not one of my finest, I forgive myself and remember that tomorrow is a new day, a new start.

Here are some tips to consider incorporating into your conditioning program.

Ask for Help

Soon after my daughter and I moved into our new home, I was in need of a handyman and called upon her friend's dad to help out with a few things. A month or so later, I bought some shelves for the garage that required assembly. She saw the boxes and excitedly sang out, "Call the handyman!" I smiled and replied, "This time I can do it myself. In fact, you and I can do it together!" She looked doubtful, but I went ahead and pulled out the hammer and the instructions, and sure enough, we were able to complete the task within just a couple of hours. Her response afterward was priceless: "Why do they call it a handyman? They should call it a handywoman!" How awesome for my daughter to see how independent and capable a woman can be!

As great as it is to demonstrate independence and competence, asking for help is good role-modeling as well. In my new life as a single parent, initially I felt very alone and isolated, and was hesitant to "bother" others with personal requests. I've since found it's not only desirable but essential to reach out to friends, handypersons, other parents, neighbors, co-workers... there was a whole network available to tap into, once my eyes were open to the possibilities.

Recently, during the morning race to get out the door in time for school and work, we got in the car and I turned the ignition – nothing. Battery's dead. Deep breath. I knew I had to exude confidence for my daughter's sake, so I said aloud for both our benefit: "Don't panic. Panic just gets in the way of clear thinking." *OK, what are my options here? If I wait for the auto club to arrive, my daughter will be way late for school, and this is an important day for her to be there. I don't have family nearby, but I do have friends. ASK FOR HELP.*

I picked up the phone and called a friend who lives nearby. As luck would have it, I caught her just as she was heading out the door to take her daughter to school, and she said YES she'd be right over to take my daughter with her, even though the girls didn't go to the same school! There she was, without hesitation, to my rescue. After she came to my aid with my daughter, I next called the auto club. They arrived relatively quickly and got the car up and running in no time at all, so in the end everything turned out just fine.

In order to ask for help, I had to get past this thing about having to be so utterly self-sufficient. I would want to be there for a friend, so why do I hesitate to reach out to one myself?

What was beautiful in the end was that this friend actually thanked *me* for reaching out to *her*. "That's what I'm here for." Thank heavens for friends. When you're like me and you don't have family around, you have to create family. That morning, I adopted a sister.

As single moms, when something unexpected happens like a car battery dying, we feel more vulnerable than ever, and feelings of helplessness and powerlessness start seeping in. NO. Refuse to let them take hold. Divert mental energy into creative thinking and determination with the belief that you can get through this, and then *make it so!*

Cast the net widely when it comes to building a support network. When I had my emergency spinal surgery, I learned in a big way the importance of reaching out for help and saying Yes to anyone who offered. I was fortunate that in addition to my small but close circle of friends, I'd also gotten to know a handful of parents of my daughter's classmates. Instead of keeping my situation private, which was my natural tendency, I opened up and shared my story with a couple of them. They generously offered to add their names to my support list, and I humbly accepted. It was challenging for me, but I had to surrender to the fact that I just couldn't do everything myself. I needed help.

There's another part of the equation that hasn't yet been addressed: asking for help not because we *need* it, but because we *want* it. Even if I *can* do everything myself (I am superwoman, after all), there may be times that I *want* help, and there's nothing wrong with that (still convincing myself of this, but I've come a long way). Maybe I need to run some errands, and having my daughter in tow is just not the best way to go. Or maybe I simply want a couple of hours to myself (how selfish!). That's when the beauty of parents helping parents comes into play, a healthy and mutually satisfying give-and-take. A fellow parent can take my daughter for a couple of hours this time, and next time I'll take theirs. It's a win-win situation for all involved – especially the children, who benefit from extra play dates!

I tend to take such pride in being independent and need-free, but today I know that's a self-defeating position to embrace. *So What* if I ask for help. There's no shame in this. And the person can decline if it's a hardship for them.

I don't have to anticipate everyone else's needs and put theirs before mine. They're fully capable of setting their own boundaries and saying *no*, just like I am.

Take Time without Guilt

Take time for self care. Take a day off just because. Easier said than done, that's for sure, but definitely worth the effort.

When there's a partner or someone else around the house available to help out, we can take a time out and let that other person take the lead when we feel our energy is spent or the volcano is beginning to erupt. But when we're on our own, it's non-stop action without any breaks, and it can be just plain exhausting. This pace takes a toll not only on our mental health, but on our physical health as well. It's not just a suggestion, it's a requirement: Choose to take downtime for yourself, or else your body may make the choice for you.

I am allowed to have a life of my own in addition to parenting. I am allowed to enjoy coffee with a friend or relish hours of solitude when my daughter is away at her dad's. It doesn't mean I'm not totally dedicated to her or that I love her any less than completely. It just means that I need to honor and fill my own needs as fully as I honor and fill hers.

As sociable and extraverted as I may appear, there's a deep-rooted hermit inside me that desperately requires cave time. When I go too long without nourishing this hermit, it can get ugly. I become unhappy, irritable and impatient, and inevitably end up snapping more frequently at my daughter. While my own personal need is for hermit time, yours may be for more social time and to go out dancing with friends. Whatever your particular need may be, make that time for yourself, *guilt-free.*

Write It Out

A remarkable thing has transpired for me during the writing of this book. I've found that the more I write about my experiences with *So What*, the more forgiving and at peace with myself I become. This is no big surprise, really... I'm a big fan of exploring my inner world through writing in a journal, and writing this book has been a similar process for me. If you don't already maintain a journal, I encourage you to consider trying it out. Find a special blank book in which you can start writing your own experiences and ways of applying *So What* in your world. Write about the successes as well as the challenges and frustrations. When times are rough, re-read the successes and remind yourself about forgiveness, and comfort yourself as you would comfort a friend. Writing can help you find your center again and give you strength to take on a new day.

Here are some questions to ask yourself when encountered with a *So What* opportunity:

Where is this stress/anxiety coming from?

Is one of my buttons or hooks being triggered?

Is it concern about what others will think?

Is it shame for not following the rules laid out when I was growing up?

Is it some kind of futuristic fear factor where I'm trying to protect and control all angles?

Or is my response coming from my core values and beliefs, so I'm not going to let this one go?

There is no right way to write. If writing in a book isn't your thing, use your keyboard instead. When you take time to write, you're also taking time for yourself. Bonus!

Come to Your Senses

As I've mentioned time and again throughout these pages, the power of *So What* lies in our ability to get present, in order to tap into our creative energy and respond in the moment. Here's a simple little 5-senses centering exercise that takes just one minute to complete, and can be performed anytime, anywhere.

Begin with a deep breath, and then...

Look. Observe shapes... colors... patterns.

Listen. Perceive sounds... the ticking of a clock... the hum of traffic.

Smell. Take another deep breath and take in the various scents in your environment.

Taste. Move your tongue and sense the flavor of your mouth.

Touch. Experience different textures... the sleeve of your shirt, the back of your hand.

Now take one more deep breath, and notice how much more relaxed and present you feel.

Tackle the What-If's

Earlier I noted that anxiety is an emotion based in the future, the land of uncertainty. We get into a worried state when we allow our mind to imagine the universe of possibilities that haven't even happened yet. *What-If* is the trigger that sets off this pattern of thinking. Taming our *What-If's* is the key to alleviating anxiety and transporting our mind back to the present.

Remember, we may not have control over the events in our lives, but we do have control over the way we choose to view and respond to them. We have the power to put a new frame on any picture, especially one that hasn't yet been developed. The following activity is a great place to start.

Get out a piece of lined paper and draw a vertical line down the middle of it.

In the left column, flush out a list of all your *What-If's*, all those unknowns that generate fear and anxiety. Try to fill the entire page; write until you feel completely spent. Examples of some *What-If's* to stimulate your own:

What If I pick the wrong school?

What If she breaks her arm learning how to skateboard?

What If she falls into the wrong crowd?

Now, in the right column, respond to each *What-If* with a practical *If-Then*:

What If I pick the wrong school?

If I pick the wrong school, *then* I'll transfer her to another one.

What If she breaks her arm learning how to skateboard?

If she breaks her arm, *then* she'll have a cast on it for a while.

What If she falls into the wrong crowd?

If she falls into the wrong crowd, *then*...

Hmm...

Sometimes we get stuck. When we can't find a satisfactory *If-Then* for a *What-If*, we can always fall back on the old faithful adage, *we'll cross that bridge when we get to it.*

What-If shines the spotlight on uncertainty by leaving the questions open-ended; *If-Then* diffuses the anxious glare by subtly closing the questions.

Nothing gets accomplished by worrying about the abundance of *What-If's* that may await our children and us. The present is all that's real. Turn *What-If's* into *If-Then's*, and then *So What.*

The trick is to let go of fear and have faith that somehow, some way, we'll get through whatever life has to deal, even though at times it feels so overwhelming and exhausting. We've made it this far... we can go the distance.

Engage an Ally

Share this book with a friend who's in a similar boat, and talk about the ideas that particularly speak to you. Set weekly or monthly dates to exchange stories about your successes and challenges.

When we team up with a fellow traveler, an invisible weight lifts. It's amazing how much relief there can be in discovering we're not alone. A fresh perspective, whether it fits or not, can unlock the brain from being stuck in a futile, repetitive cycle, opening our mind's eye to new avenues. Talking with a friend may even provide an opportunity to *laugh* about our difficulties, which is the best stress relief of all!

Reprise

It's no easy thing to stay sane in insane times. But with adequate self-care, some levity and a healthy *So What* approach to life, it can be done.

Since incorporating *So What* into my being, the metamorphosis has been astonishing. My daughter and I have come so far in such a relatively short amount of time, due primarily to my new attitude and her responsiveness. According to the hypothetical Age Standards chart, she's too young to be getting this many choices and to have such freedom. But when I throw out the chart and just pay attention to this young person in front of me, I feel completely confident in the approach I'm taking with her. This is the 21st century and I'm a single mom. It's time to adjust to the modern era and reconsider The Rules that were ingrained in me and still reside in the deepest recesses of my soul.

I am not a "bad" mom. I'm a COURAGEOUS mom. I have the courage to blaze my own trail as I parent this precious gem of a child. *So What* if the "others" judge me harshly. These others are mostly just figments of my childhood imagination. Today, I choose more loving and accepting figments, thank you very much. And I encourage you to do the same.

***

So What is about learning how to let go of both the inner and outer struggle.

It's about forgiveness of imperfection.

It's about letting go of some (not all) control.

It's about letting go of fear and guilt – emotions rooted in the illusion of the future and remnants of the past.

It's about coming back to the here-and-now, to what's real.

Ultimately, it's about fostering that precious bond between you and your child.

When the day-to-day stuff of life derails us, *So What* helps to restore our sanity and get us back on track.

Appreciations

Thank you, Lisa, for being my champion long before the book ever reached your hands, and for your unwavering encouragement and support from the moment it did.

Thank you, Bev, for the extraordinary amount of time and attention you gave to this project, and for your gentle and spirit-filled way of helping to shape my words without shaping my message.

Thank you, Aimee, for your astute and inspiring professional and personal feedback.

Thank you, Shannon, for your enthusiastic response and perceptive comments.

Thank you, Wayne, for being there with invaluable reflections as friend and mentor.

Thank you, my dear sisters Marcie and Ariel, for your unique and thoughtful perspectives.

Above all, thank you, Liana, for your abundant love and generous permission to share our personal stories with others.